The Night with the Dinosaurs

Happy House

About Wise & Wide

- A systematic 6-level English reading program based on Lexile® measures
- Diverse and interesting topics chosen from the elementary curriculums of Korea and English speaking western countries
- Well-written books in various forms including fiction stories, descriptive texts, and classics retold
- The informative but original fiction stories grab your interest, leading to the easy and clear understanding of the educational content.
- Improve thinking skills with solid after-reading activities at all levels of the series.

Wise & Wide is a 6-level English reading program that consists of 60 books and each level is systematically divided by Lexile® measures. The Lexile® Framework for Reading is the most popular reading measuring system in American formal education curriculums and many English programs. Over 20 out of 50 states in the U.S. mark Lexile® measures directly on students' final report cards and over 300 well-known publishers adopt and use Lexile® measures.

Experience many kinds of readings written by professional writers from the U.S. and England. They used interesting topics that were carefully chosen after analyzing elementary curriculums from around the world including Korea, the U.S., England, and Australia among many others. Comprehensive after-reading activities including graphic organizers, speaking tasks, and After-reading Tests are ready for you.

Levels in the series and their corresponding Lexile® measures

Level	Lexile® measures	U.S. Grade
Level 1	Below 200L	Pre K - K
Level 2	190L - 400L	Lower Grade 1
Level 3	350L - 530L	Upper Grade 1
Level 4	420L - 650L	Grade 2
Level 5	520L - 940L	Grade 3 - 4
Level 6	830L - 1070L	Grade 5 - 6

* Smart Readers: Wise & Wide level 1 is applicable to the preschool level in the U.S.

* The source of the relationship between Lexile® measures and U.S. school grades: CCSS(Common Core State Standards) FOR ENGLISH LANGUAGE ARTS, APPENDIX A (2012, which is used by 45 states in the U.S.)

Topic List

	Level 1	Level 2	Level 3	Level 4	Level 5	Level 6
Book 1	Science>Biology: The hibernation of animals Story	Science>Biology: Living and nonliving things Story	Science>Biology> Animals & the Environment: Sea otters Story	Environment> Living with nature: The diver & the persimmon tree Story	Science>Biology> Animal: Amazing animals of the Amazon Story	Science>Biology: Germs, transmitted diseases Story
Book 2	Literature> World classics: Aesop's fables Story	Literature> Traditional fairy tale: Old tales about stones Story	Social Studies> Economy: To run a business to make and save money Story	Science>Biology> Plants: Photosynthesis Story	Science>Earth science: Earth's layers,earthquakes, volcanoes, and earth's atmosphere Report	Mathematics> Sequence: The golden ratio & the Fibonacci sequence Story
Book 3	Science>Physics: How shadows are formed Story	Literature> World classics: Peter Pan Story	Science>Scientific technology: Nanobots Story	Literature>Myths: World's creation stories Story	Literature> Legend: The story of King Arthur Story	Literature>Myths: Constellation myths Story
Book 4	Literature> Traditional literature: The Talmud Story	Science>Biology> Animal: Polar bears Story	Science>Biology> Animal: Mountain gorillas Story	Social Studies> Cultural anthropology: Amazing ancient cultures of the world Story	Science> Earth science: Clouds and weather Story	Literature> Human & animals: The friendship between a girl and a horse Story
Book 5	Social Studies> Ethics: Rules in daily life Story	Science>Biology: The five senses Report	Social Studies> Cultural anthropology: Astonishing festivals Report	Art>Music: Stories from two operas Story	Social Studies> World culture & history: The Renaissance Story	
Book 6	Social Studies> World geography & travel: Tourist attractions around the world Story	Science>Biology> Animal: Dinosaurs Story	Science> Astronomy: The solar system Story	Social Studies> People: Three great people who overcame hardships Story	Science>Scientific technology: The wonderful world of robots Report	
Book 7		Social Studies> Cultural anthropology: Mythological monsters from around the world Report		Science & Social Studies> Technology & culture: Inventions from around the world Report	Art>Works of art: Famous paintings Report	
Book 8				Social Studies> History: The California Gold Rush Report	Social Studies & Science> Psychology: Psychology in everyday life Story	
Book 9						
Book 10						

* 10 books in each level will be published.

How to Use This Book

•Before Reading

You can easily find the topic and what kind of story you are about to read.

•The text

All the stories were written by professional writers from the U.S. and England, so you will read authentic and appropriate English sentences and expressions in every book in the series.

•Pop Quiz

Check out right away if you understand what you have just read by solving a pop quiz that checks your comprehension.

•Key Words

The key words and expressions on each page are listed for you to easily study them.

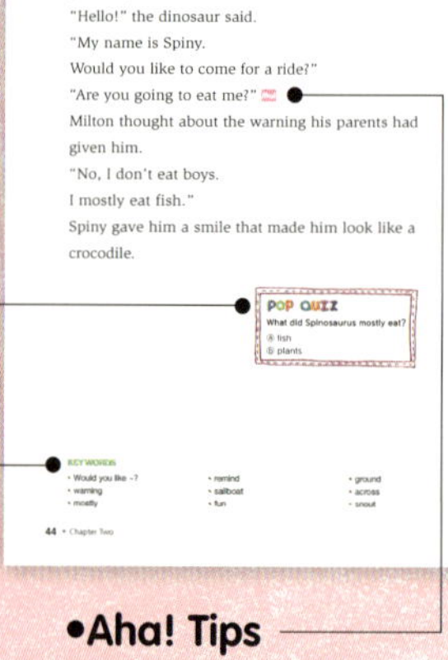

•Aha! Tips

Download free Korean explanations at *www.ihappyhouse.co.kr* for all of the sentences marked with "Aha!". These explain cultural, scientific, and economic knowledge or they deal with aspects of English such as grammatical structures or idiomatic expressions. There are lots of "Aha! Tips" to help you understand the text.

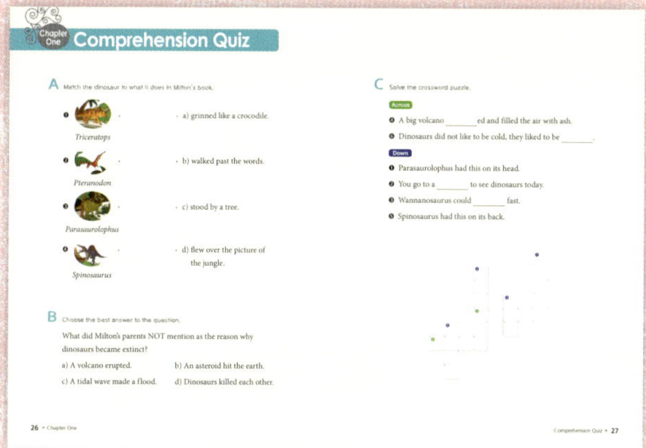

•Comprehension Quiz

After reading one chapter, solve various questions to find out if you fully understand the content.

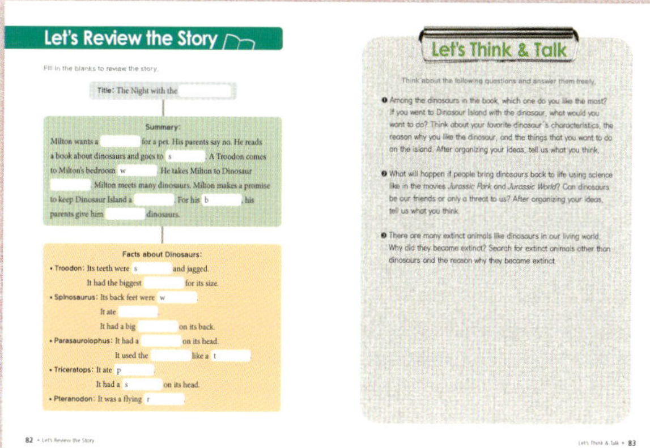

•Let's Review the Story /
•Let's Think & Talk

Fill in the blanks in the organizer to summarize the whole story. Express your own thinking and feelings about the story by answering the questions. You can build up logic and reasoning skills for your essay examinations in the future.

Appendix

Audio CD

In the CD audio book form, the texts are read vividly by American professional voice actors.

After-reading Test

Solve an additionally provided After-reading Test for each book.

The Korean translation, Answer Keys, a Word Quiz, a Word List, and Aha! Tips for each book

You can download them for free at *www.ihappyhouse.co.kr*

Before Reading

The Night with the Dinosaurs

Level 2–6,
Lexile®330L

•Science〉Biology〉Animal
•Story

The dinosaur, a mysterious friend of children!

The most loved animal of children is the dinosaur! The word "dinosaur" is Greek in origin and it means "scary lizard." The first person who used the word "dinosaur" is Richard Owen, an English paleontologist. Dinosaurs are reptiles like crocodiles and turtles. They are animals that lived during the Mesozoic era. It is said that their sizes varied from 30 centimeters to 40 meters. At that time, there were pterosaurs that flew in the sky and ichthyosaurs that lived in the sea. But, as a matter of fact, neither of those animals can be called dinosaurs. Dinosaurs must live on land.

Dinosaurs are divided into two types: herbivores, which ate plants, and carnivores, which ate meat. It is said that carnivorous dinosaurs like the Tyrannosaurus attacked herbivorous dinosaurs or other animal, so herbivorous dinosaurs like the Triceratops were always tense as they had to protect themselves from carnivorous dinosaurs.

Summary

Milton, a cute and goofy boy who loves dinosaurs!

One night before going to bed, Milton asked his mom and dad if he could raise a dinosaur as a pet. His mom and dad responded to his ridiculous request by saying that he couldn't raise a dinosaur as a pet because dinosaurs didn't exist anymore. Disappointed, Milton read a pop-up dinosaur book so that he could meet dinosaurs in his dream. After falling asleep, Milton woke up when he heard strange sounds coming through the window. Rubbing his sleepy eyes, Milton looked out the window and right into another pair of eyes.

Whose eyes were they? What was outside? What will happen to Milton?

Contents

The Night with the Dinosaurs

The Night with
the Dinosaurs

Chapter One

Milton Wants a Dinosaur

"Mom, may I have a pet?"

Milton really, really wanted a pet.

"Yes, you may." Mom smiled.

"What kind of pet do you want?

Do you want a dog?"

"No, not a dog."

Milton shook his head.

"How about a cat?"

"No, not a cat."

"A hamster?"

"No, not a hamster.

There is one pet that I really, really want," Milton

said. Aha!

▲ hamster

KEY WORDS

- dinosaur
- May I ~? (*cf.* may)
- have a pet (have-had-had)
- what kind of
- shake one's head (shake-shook-shaken)
- How about ~?
- hamster

"I can't guess," said Dad.

"What kind of pet do you want, Milton?"

Milton crossed his fingers.

"I really, really, really want a dinosaur for a pet.

May I please have a dinosaur?"

Mom frowned.

Dad rubbed his nose.

Milton's parents both shook their heads.

"No, you cannot have a dinosaur," Mom told him.

"Dinosaurs are extinct.

They all died a long time ago."

▲ cross one's fingers

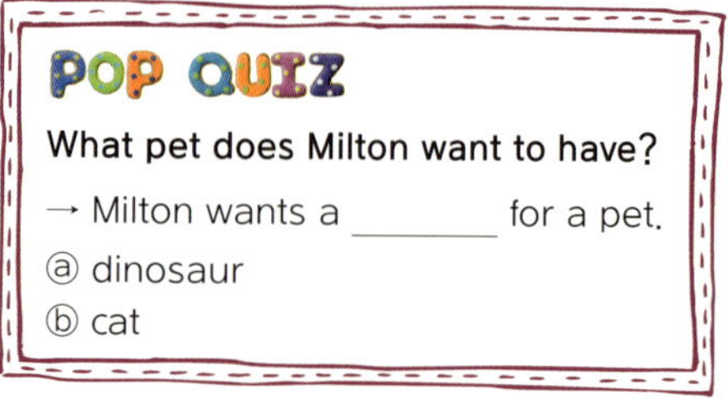

KEY WORDS

- can't[cannot] + *Verb* (↔ can + *Verb*)
- guess
- cross one's fingers
- frown
- rub
- parent
- both
- **tell** (tell-told-told)
- extinct
- die
- a long time ago

"How did they all die?" Milton asked.

"Perhaps a big volcano erupted and filled the air with ash," Dad said.

"Perhaps an asteroid hit Earth. It may have killed them," Mom told Milton. "It would have made a big explosion."

"An asteroid?

What is that?" Milton asked.

"An asteroid is a rock that is in outer space.

Some people think one hit our planet," explained

Mom.

"Maybe both things happened," said Dad.

"It is possible an asteroid landed in an ocean and

a volcano erupted."

▲ an asteroid flying to Earth

- perhaps
- volcano
- erupt
- fill
- ash
- asteroid
- hit (hit-hit-hit)
- Earth (= the earth)
- kill
- explosion
- rock
- outer space
- planet
- explain
- maybe
- happen
- possible (↔ impossible)
- land
- ocean

"The asteroid would have made big tidal waves.
The ocean water would have flooded the land,"
Mom told him.

"The ash from the volcano would have gone into
the air.
It would have made big, windy storms," Dad told
him.

"All the ash in the air would have made big clouds.
It would have made the earth cold," Mom said.

"Dinosaurs liked to be warm," Dad said.

"If it had been too cold, they would have died."

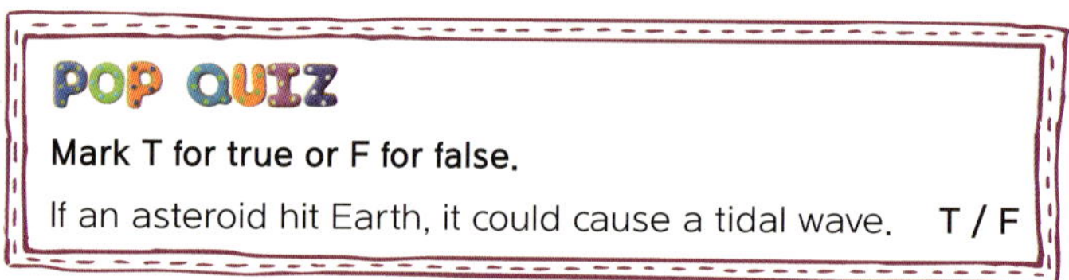

KEY WORDS

- tidal wave
- flood
- windy
- storm
- cloud
- cold (↔ warm)
- if
- too
- see (see-saw-seen)

- only
- place
- museum
- scientist
- put together (put-put-put)
- bone
- know (know-knew-known)
- look like

"That's sad," Milton said.

"I really, really, really want to see a dinosaur."

"There is only one place to see a dinosaur today,"
Dad said.

"That is in a museum.

Scientists put dinosaur bones together.

That's how we know what they looked like."

"But what if they are not extinct?" Milton asked.

"What if dinosaurs still live somewhere?

Then may I have one as a pet?"

Mom and Dad shook their heads.

"That is not possible."

"Why?" Milton asked.

"I will take the best care of my dinosaur."

"No. Playing with a dinosaur is a very, very, very

bad idea," Dad tucked Milton into his bed.

"Read your dinosaur book.

Then go to sleep."

Mom kissed Milton on the cheek.

"Sweet dreams."

They left the bedroom.

KEY WORDS

- What if ~?
- still
- somewhere
- then
- as
- take care of (take-took-taken)
- best
- tuck
- go to sleep (go-went-gone) (*cf.* sleep (sleep-slept-slept))
- kiss + *a person* + on the cheek
- Sweet dreams. (*cf.* dream)
- leave (leave-left-left)

Milton opened his pop-up dinosaur book.

A Pteranodon spread its wings on the page.

It flew over the picture of the jungle.

A Triceratops walked past the words.

It looked big and heavy.

KEY WORDS

- pop-up book
- Pteranodon
- **spread** (spread-spread-spread)
- wing
- **fly** (fly-flew-flown)
- over
- jungle
- Triceratops
- walk
- past
- heavy

A Tyrannosaurus stood up with its mouth open, ready to roar.

A Spinosaurus grinned like a crocodile.

It was the biggest dinosaur on the page.

It had a big sail on top of its back.

KEY WORDS

- Tyrannosaurus
- **stand up** (stand-stood-stood)
- ready
- roar

- Spinosaurus
- grin
- crocodile
- biggest

- sail
- on top of
- back

A Parasaurolophus stood by a tree.

It had a red crest.

Milton had watched

a video about

Parasaurolophus.

It showed the dinosaur

used its crest to make

trumpet sounds.

▲ trumpet

He looked at the picture of a Troodon.

It was a small dinosaur, only about one meter tall.

The smallest dinosaur in his book was

Wannanosaurus.

It was only the size of a chicken.

It could run fast.

Milton thought that was a good thing.

KEY WORDS

- Parasaurolophus
- by
- crest
- trumpet
- sound
- Troodon

- meter (1 m = 100 cm)
- smallest
- Wannanosaurus
- could
- run (run-ran-run)
- think (think-thought-thought)

Milton listened to the quiet night.

His eyes grew heavy.

He held his book on his chest.

He drifted off to sleep.

Pteranodon

It is a pterosaur that flew in the sky. Its name means "it has wings, but no teeth." It is said that its wings were about 8 meters long when they were spread out and it hunted fish while living on a sea cliff.

Triceratops

It means "three-horned face" in Greek. This dinosaur had a horn on its nose and two horns on its forehead, and a big frill around its neck. It looked similar to a rhinoceros. It was a herbivorous dinosaur whose body was 6~9 meters long.

Tyrannosaurus

The Tyrannosaurus is also known as the Tyrannosaurus Rex or T-Rex. It is known as the most ferocious and scariest dinosaur among carnivorous dinosaurs. The name also means "tyrant lizard." Its body was 12~13 meters long and it had a big skull compared to the size of its body. It was a carnivorous dinosaur that walked on two feet.

Spinosaurus

It was one of the biggest carnivorous dinosaurs and its name means "spine lizard." It had a sail in the shape of the ribs of a fan growing on its back and it had the longest body among carnivorous dinosaurs. Some people have claimed that its body was around 18 meters long.

Parasaurolophus

It means "near crested lizard" because it was similar to a crested lizard. It was a herbivorous dinosaur that had a 2-meter-long crest in the shape of a long pipe on the back of its head. It is said that it hid under the water when it faced danger.

Troodon

It means "wounding tooth." It was a small carnivorous dinosaur that was more like a bird than a reptile. It had the biggest brain compared to its body among dinosaurs, so it seemed to be smart.

A Match the dinosaur to what it does in Milton's book.

 ❶ 

Triceratops

❷ 

Pteranodon

❸ 

Parasaurolophus

 ❹ 

Spinosaurus

- a) grinned like a crocodile.

- b) walked past the words.

- c) stood by a tree.

- d) flew over the picture of the jungle.

B Choose the best answer to the question.

What did Milton's parents NOT mention as the reason why dinosaurs became extinct?

a) A volcano erupted.

b) An asteroid hit the earth.

c) A tidal wave made a flood.

d) Dinosaurs killed each other.

Solve the crossword puzzle.

Across

❹ A big volcano __________ ed and filled the air with ash.

❻ Dinosaurs did not like to be cold, they liked to be __________ .

Down

❶ Parasaurolophus had this on its head.

❷ You go to a __________ to see dinosaurs today.

❸ Wannanosaurus could __________ fast.

❺ Spinosaurus had this on its back.

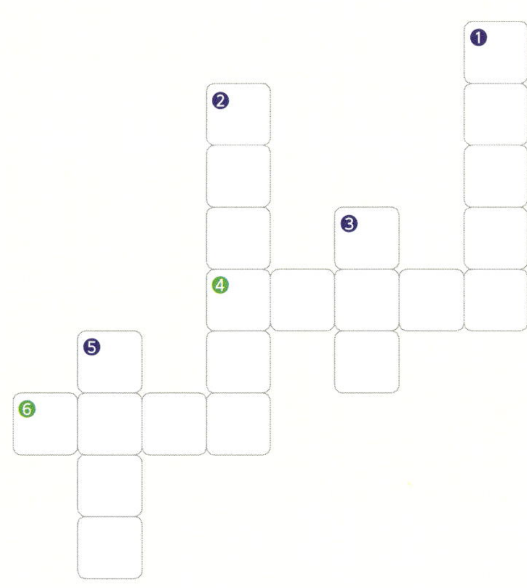

Playing with Dinosaurs

"Scratch! Scratch! Scrape!"

A noise at the window woke up Milton.

It was still dark.

The noise was outside.

He heard the trees move.

Was it the wind?

He saw a shadow cross his window.

Was it a cloud covering the moon?

A trumpet sounded far away.

He heard a roar in the distance.

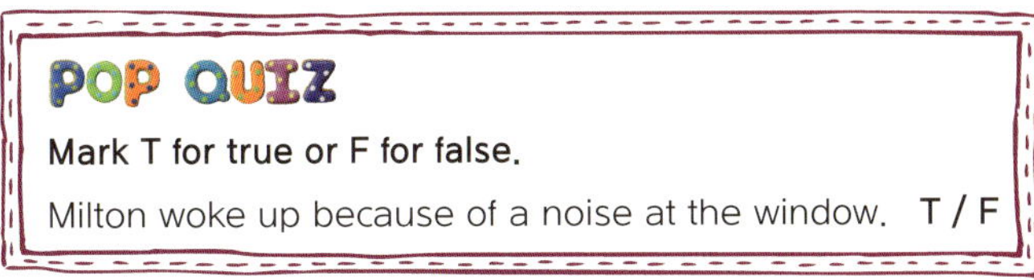

KEY WORDS

- **scratch** (*cf.* scrape)
- **noise**
- **wake up** (wake-woke-woken)
- **outside** (↔ inside)
- **hear** (hear-heard-heard)
- **shadow**
- **cross**
- **cover** (*cf.* the covers)
- **far away** (*cf.* far)
- **in the distance**

Milton threw back the covers.

He jumped out of bed.

He put on his slippers and his robe.

He opened the window shade.

Blink! Blink!

Two eyes peered in the window at Milton.

"Who are you?" Milton asked.

"I am a Troodon.

My name is Tory."

He growled softly.

He sounded like a cat purring.

He smiled.

He had many sharp teeth with jagged edges.

KEY WORDS

- **throw back** (throw-threw-thrown)
- **jump out of bed**
- **put on**
- **slipper**
- **robe**
- **window shade**
- **blink**

- **peer**
- **growl**
- **softly**
- **purr**
- **sharp**
- **jagged**
- **edge**

Milton rubbed his eyes.

Was he dreaming? **Aha!**

How did a dinosaur come to his house?

"Can you come out to play?" the Troodon asked.

Milton remembered what Dad had told him.

"Playing with a dinosaur is a very, very, very bad idea."

But Milton really, really, really liked dinosaurs.

Milton smiled at the Troodon.

It looked friendly.

"I'll be outside in one minute," he whispered.

KEY WORDS

- come out to + *Verb* (come-came-come)
- remember
- friendly
- minute
- whisper
- another

- poke
- bush
- shield
- wait
- chomp (on)
- leaves

Then another dinosaur poked its head out of the
bushes.

It had a big shield on its head.

It was a Triceratops!

"Okay! We'll wait!"

The Triceratops said, and chomped on some leaves.

Milton opened his bedroom door.

He peeked in the hallway.

He peeked in Mom and Dad's bedroom.

Dad snored. Mom was sleeping, too.

He tiptoed down the hall, to the kitchen, out the back door, and into the deep, dark night.

"Come on," said Tory.

The Troodon hopped on his big hind legs.

Tory opened the gate.

The Troodon was about 1.5 meters tall.

"I thought most dinosaurs were big," Milton said.

"Some dinosaurs are big.

Spinosaurus is in the lake and he is a giant.

Tyrannosaurus Rex is huge."

Tory hopped to the front yard.

"Some dinosaurs are very small."

"Are you talking about me?"

A small dinosaur sat
by the gate.

It had a hard shell.

KEY WORDS

- peek in
- hallway (*cf.* hall)
- snore
- tiptoe
- down
- back door
- deep
- Come on!
- hop
- hind leg
- gate
- most
- lake
- giant
- huge
- front yard
- sit (sit-sat-sat)
- hard
- shell

Milton bent down and tapped his hand on her shell.

"Who are you?" Milton asked.

"I am Proganochelys," she told him.

"You look like a turtle!" Milton said.

"Do I?" the dinosaur asked.

"Yes. Except you have spikes on your neck. You have a sharp tail, too."

An insect scurried by.

Proganochelys ate it.

Tory pointed a claw at his chest.

"I am small, but I am the smartest!"

Milton said, "I read in a book that you are smarter than any other dinosaur."

"That is a good book!"

Tory made a happy growl.

"My brain is bigger than any other dinosaur's brain for my size.

Let's go play!" **Aha!**

The Troodon hopped down the street.

Milton had to run to keep up with him.

"Where are we going?"

"We are going to a secret place," Tory told him.

Triceratops lumbered next to them.

"Do you want a ride, Milton?"

"Yes, please."

Milton climbed up on the dinosaur's tail.

"Thank you, Triceratops."

"You can call me Cera."

Milton climbed from Cera's tail to his neck.

It was eight meters long.

Cera was three meters tall.

Milton felt like he was standing on a mountain.

Cera was just tall enough to eat a branch of a pine tree. **Aha!**

So Cera did just that.

Boom. Boom. Boom.

The sidewalk shook with every step Cera took.

Milton held on to the bony shield on Cera's head.

He did not want to fall.

▲ pine tree

KEY WORDS

- lumber
- next to
- **ride** (ride-rode-ridden)
- climb up on
- call
- mountain
- just
- enough

- branch
- pine tree
- boom
- sidewalk
- every
- take a step
- hold on to
- bony

Cera stopped to eat some roses from Mrs. Green's garden.

"Mrs. Green keeps complaining about a deer eating her roses," Milton said.

"I think you are the one eating them!"

Cera nodded and swallowed the flowers.

"Yum, yum."

Next, he went to
Mr. Brown's magnolia bush.
He ate the leaves.
He ate the flowers.
Then he moved on to a fig
tree.
"The most delicious plants
grow on your street," Cera
said.
"People think that because
I'm big, I eat meat.
But I only eat plants."

▲ magnolia

▲ fig

POP QUIZ

Circle the right word for the underlined part.

Triceratops ate some (lilies / roses).

KEY WORDS

- Mrs.
- garden
- keep
- complain
- deer
- nod
- swallow
- yum
- Mr.
- magnolia
- move on to
- fig tree
- delicious
- plant
- because
- meat

At last they came to a lake.

A huge fin rose out of the lake.

It looked like a sail as it moved back and forth in

the water.

Milton's eyes popped open.

"What a big shark!"

KEY WORDS

- at last
- fin
- rise (rise-rose-risen)
- back and forth
- pop
- shark

Tory laughed.

"No, it is much bigger than a shark's fin.

It is a Spinosaurus' sail.

He is coming to play."

KEY WORDS

- laugh

A long neck with a mouth like a crocodile's
poked up from the water.

"Hello!" the dinosaur said.

"My name is Spiny.

Would you like to come for a ride?"

"Are you going to eat me?" Aha!

Milton thought about the warning his parents had
given him.

"No, I don't eat boys.

I mostly eat fish."

Spiny gave him a smile that made him look like a
crocodile.

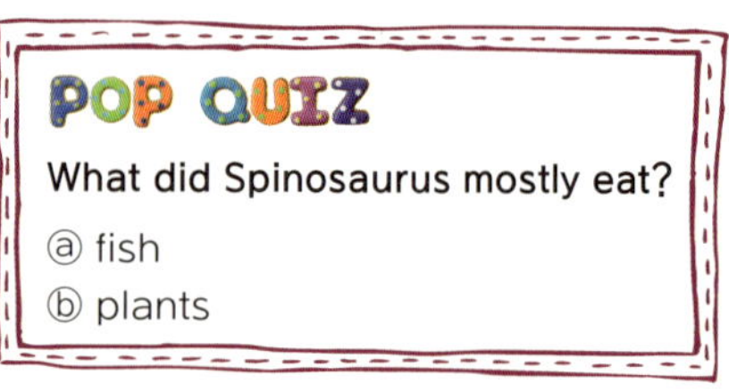

KEY WORDS

- Would you like ~?
- warning
- mostly

- remind
- sailboat
- fun

- ground
- across
- snout

Spiny's sail reminded Milton of a big sailboat.

It would be fun to go for a ride.

"Yes, I would like a ride!" he told the huge

Spinosaurus.

Spiny put his head on the ground.

Milton climbed across the dinosaur's long snout.

He walked across his long neck.

He held on to Spiny's sail.

Tory hopped on, too.

Cera nodded goodbye to them.

"You go ahead. Have fun.

I'm going to stay here and eat some leaves."

They sped across the water.

The wind blew Milton's hair.

"How do you swim so fast?" he asked.

"My back feet are webbed," Spiny told him.

"They help me in the water.

But I have big claws on my front feet.

I use them to dig in the mud and to catch fish."

They swam across the lake into the fog.

The fog was thick.

The sky was dark.

Milton could not see.

"Are we lost?" Milton asked.

"No, we are not lost," Tory told him.

"The fog hides our secret place."

KEY WORDS

- nod goodbye to
- go ahead
- have fun
- stay
- speed (speed-sped-sped)
- blow (blow-blew-blown)
- feet
- webbed

- dig (dig-dug-dug)
- mud
- catch (catch-caught-caught)
- swim (swim-swam-swum)
- fog
- thick
- lost
- hide (hide-hid-hidden)

A Choose all the words that describe the dinosaur in the middle of the picture.

a) a big sail on its back

b) a mouth like a crocodile

c) large wings

d) webbed back feet

B Choose the best answer to each question.

❶ What kind of dinosaur came to Milton's window?

a) Parasaurolophus

b) Tyrannosaurus Rex

c) Troodon

d) Spinosaurus

❷ Which was the biggest dinosaur?

a) Proganochelys

b) Troodon

c) Triceratops

d) Spinosaurus

C Solve the crossword puzzle.

❸ Cera ate some __________ from Mrs. Green's garden.

❹ Proganochelys had __________ on her neck.

❶ Troodon had many sharp __________ with jagged edges.

❷ A __________ at the window woke up Milton.

❺ Proganochelys had a hard __________ .

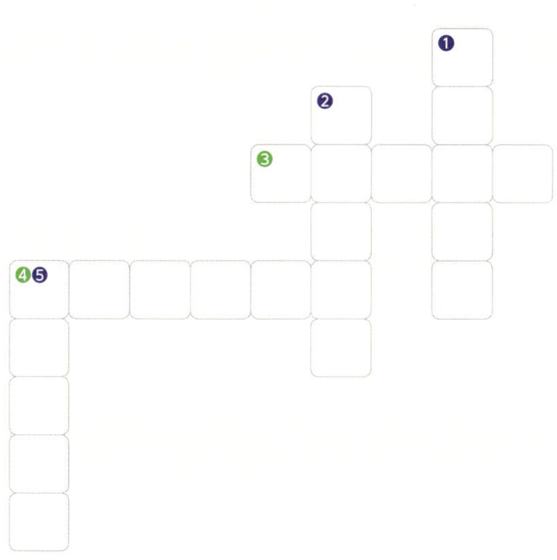

Dinosaur Island

Finally, the fog opened up.

Milton saw an island.

It had jungle plants all over.

Milton heard strange noises.

He heard screeches, rumbles, and roars.

The Spinosaurus crawled up onto the beach.

Tory hopped off Spiny's back.

He ran on the beach.

Milton slid down the thirteen-meter long tail.

He landed in the sand with a wet splat.

KEY WORDS

- island
- finally
- open up
- all over
- strange
- screech
- rumble
- crawl up

- onto
- beach
- hop off
- **slide down** (slide-slid-slid)
- sand
- wet
- splat

"Where are we?" he asked.

He did not remember ever coming to this place.

"This is our secret place," Tory told him.

"We call it Dinosaur Island.

Here we can run and play and eat and be as loud as we want." Aha!

Something flew by Milton's head.

It was only as big as a paper airplane.

KEY WORDS

- ever
- here
- loud
- something
- paper airplane
- pterosaur
- flying
- reptile
- some
- nest
- pile
- muddy

"What was that?" he asked.

"That was a pterosaur," Tory told him.

"It is not a dinosaur, and it is not a bird.

It is a flying reptile."

Spiny said, "Some of them are very small.

Some are very big."

The pterosaur flew to a nest on the ground.

Milton saw a pile of eggs in the muddy nest.

Once again, Milton heard a trumpet sound.

A three-meter tall dinosaur walked out of the trees.

It trumpeted again.

The sound came from the curved tube on its head.

It sounded like a foghorn.

"Hi, Parry," Tory said.

"This is Milton.

Milton, this is Parry." Aha!

Parry nodded her head.

Her mouth was the shape of a

duck's bill.

She had skin like a lizard.

"I like your crest," Milton told her.

"I think I heard you tonight when

I was in my bedroom."

"You probably did hear it.

I trumpet very loudly," she said.

"I like music."

"Me, too. I'll play the drums and you play a

song," Milton said.

"That sounds like fun," Parry said.

▲ a duck's bill

KEY WORDS

- once again
- come from
- curved
- tube
- foghorn
- bill
- lizard
- probably
- loudly
- play the drums (*cf.* drum)
- play a song

Milton picked up two sticks and drummed on a rock.

The Parasaurolophus trumpeted a tune.

Tory did a hopping dance.

Spiny rocked his long neck.

He waved his long tail.

He smiled like a crocodile.

"I never knew dinosaurs played music."

Milton tapped his foot.

"I never knew humans played the drums," Parry told him.

"I know another game!"

Tory jumped up and down.

"It's called fetch.

You throw the stick and I'll chase it."

Milton threw the stick as far as he could.

Tory ran fast.

He grabbed the stick with his three-fingered hand.

He brought it back to Milton.

Milton laughed and threw it again.

Tory took two big hops.

He brought the stick back again.

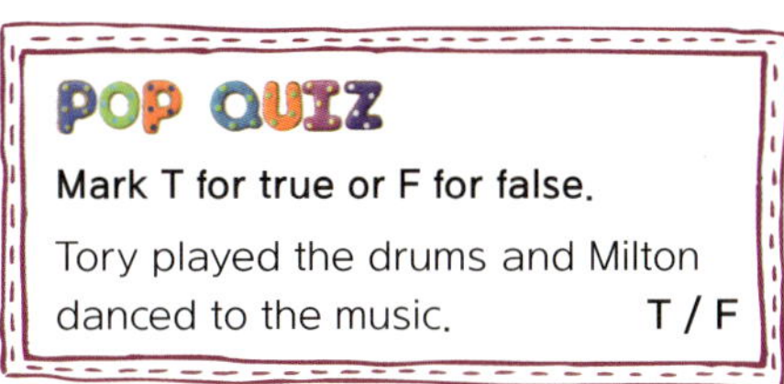

KEY WORDS

- pick up
- stick
- tune
- **do a dance** (do-did-done)
- hopping
- wave
- never

- tap one's foot
- up and down
- fetch
- chase
- grab
- three-fingered
- **bring ... back to ~** (bring-brought-brought)

A Pteranodon flew down from the treetops.

He landed beside Milton.

The Pteranodon was very big.

He was almost two meters tall, as tall as Milton's dad.

He spread his wings.

They were ten meters wide.

He was as big as a small airplane.

He waved his three small fingers.

His long finger was part of his wing.

"Do you want me to give you a ride up high in the sky?"

"Are you going to eat me?" Milton asked.

"No, I will not eat you.

I mostly eat fish."

He opened his beak.

He screeched.

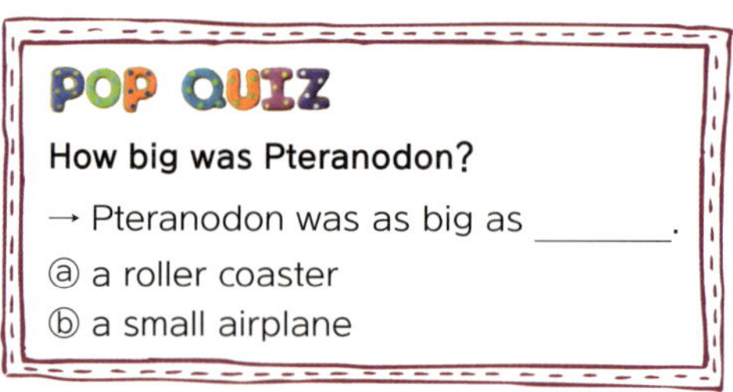

"Yes, please. I would like a ride."

Milton climbed on his back.

He put his arms around the Pteranodon's neck.

He held on tight.

They soared into the sky.

KEY WORDS

- treetop
- beside
- wide
- part of
- give a ride (give-gave-given)
- beak
- hold on tight
- soar into

Pteranodon flapped his big, leathery wings.

They flew so high Milton thought he could touch the stars.

Pteranodon flew up, down, and over the island.

It was more fun than a roller coaster ride! Aha!

Finally, they landed on the beach where Tory and Spiny waited.

They heard a rumble.

They heard a roar.

The ground shook.

Milton's legs wobbled and he fell down.

"Is that an earthquake?" he asked. Aha!

"No, it is not an earthquake.

It's Tyrannosaurus Rex!"

KEY WORDS

- flap
- leathery
- roller coaster ride
- wobble

- earthquake
- behind
- hurry
- in front of

Tory hopped behind a tree.

"Hurry and hide!

Tyrannosaurus Rex eats meat!"

Milton hid behind Tory.

He peeked out to watch the big dinosaur.

"Will he eat us?"

"Sh!"

Tory held a clawed finger in front of his mouth.

Tyrannosaurus stood tall on two feet.

He was very big.

But Spiny, the Spinosaurus was long.

He was three meters longer than the

Tyrannosaurus Rex.

Tyrannosaurus Rex roared.

His teeth were shark-like and big.

The wind from his breath blew the leaves in the

trees.

His breath smelled bad from eating meat.

"Someone needs to give T-Rex a toothbrush,"

Milton whispered to Tory.

POP QUIZ

Circle the right word for the underlined part.

Spinosaurus was (thinner / longer) than Tyrannosaurus.

KEY WORDS

- stand tall
- longer
- shark-like
- breath
- need to + *Verb*

- toothbrush
- each other
- in a circle
- go round and round
- **fight** (fight-fought-fought)

Spinosaurus roared at Tyrannosaurus Rex.

The two dinosaurs growled at each other.

They looked in each other's eyes.

They did not blink.

They both walked in a circle, round and round they went.

"Are they going to fight?" Milton asked.

"I don't know. We have to stay quiet."

Tory stayed behind the tree.

Spiny's sail turned a bright color.

He opened his mouth and showed his giant, slanted teeth.

Tyrannosaurus Rex lifted his head to the sky and roared one more time.

His loud roar hurt Milton's ears.

Spiny backed into the water of the lake.

He still watched Tyrannosaurus Rex.

Tyrannosaurus Rex followed Spiny.

He stopped at the edge of the water.

Tory and Milton watched the big dinosaur roar
one more time.
Then he turned and walked back into the jungle.
Trees crashed to the ground.
The ground shook with his steps.

KEY WORDS

- bright
- slanted
- lift

- one more time
- hurt (hurt-hurt-hurt)
- back into

- follow
- crash

"That was a close call," Milton whispered.

"It's getting late.

We should take you home."

Tory was already on Spiny's back.

"Come on, Milton.

The sun will come up soon."

Milton wished they could stay longer.

But he knew Tory was right.

Spiny put his head on the beach.

Milton climbed on his back.

He held on to the sail.

They raced across the lake to the other beach.

KEY WORDS

- close call
- get (get-got-gotten)
- late
- should + *Verb*
- take
- already
- come up
- soon
- wish
- right
- race

Comprehension Quiz

A Circle the character which said each line.

❶ "I trumpet very loudly." **Tory / Parry**

❷ "Tyrannosaurus Rex eats meat!" **Tory / Parry**

B Solve the crossword puzzle.

Across

❸ Milton saw eggs in the __________.

❹ Spinosaurus smiled like a __________.

❺ Pteranodon mostly ate __________.

Down

❶ Milton played __________ with Tory.

❷ Milton drummed on a __________.

❶ Which dinosaur had a curved tube like a trumpet on its head?

a) Pterosaur

b) Pteranodon

c) Parasaurolophus

d) Proganochelys

❷ What is NOT true about Pteranodon?

a) Pteranodon was as tall as Milton's dad.

b) Pteranodon's wings were two meters wide.

c) Pteranodon was as big as a small airplane.

d) Pteranodon's longer finger was part of its wing.

❸ What happened when Tyrannosaurus walked?

a) The ground felt as if an earthquake was happening.

b) The ground cracked open.

c) The dust rose from the ground.

d) Tyrannosaurus Rex made holes in the ground.

Saying Goodbye

Tory walked Milton back to his house.

Milton opened the gate.

"Why don't you stay here with me?

You could be my pet."

Tory shook his head.

"That would be a very, very, very bad idea."

"Why? I really, really, really want a dinosaur.

Will you come to school with me?"

"I cannot come to school with you.

I would have to be quiet.

Dinosaurs do not like to be quiet."

"Then will you visit me at recess?

We can play jump rope."

"I cannot play jump rope with you at recess.

I will scare the other children."

"You can help me with my homework.

You are very smart."

"No, I cannot help you with your homework.

My claws are too long to hold a pencil. Aha!

They will tear the paper."

Milton sighed.

"Then may I come visit you at Dinosaur Island

again?"

"You may. We will come pick you up one night,"

Troodon told him.

"However, you must never, ever, ever tell anyone

about the island. It is a secret."

"I can keep a secret."

Milton crossed his heart with his finger.

That sealed the promise.

Secret!

"If grown-ups find out about our island, they will try to trap us."

"Why?"

"They will put us in a zoo."

"In a zoo?"

Milton frowned.

"You wouldn't be able to run free and wild."

"That is why you must keep Dinosaur Island a secret.

You must never tell anyone about it."

Milton nodded.

He yawned.

His long night had made him sleepy.

"I promise."

KEY WORDS

- grown-up
- **find out** (find-found-found)
- try to + *Verb*
- trap
- be able to + *Verb*
- free
- wild
- yawn
- sleepy
- through
- pull down

He waved goodbye to Troodon and went to his
room.

He watched through the window as Troodon
hopped away.

Milton pulled down the shade and went to sleep.

He dreamed of Dinosaur Island.

Snap!

His mom pulled up the window shade.

"Wake up, sleepyhead!"

The room filled with sunlight.

Milton rubbed his eyes.

Mom and Dad stood by his bed.

They smiled.

"Happy birthday!"

Dad rubbed Milton's head.

"We have a surprise for you."

"Come into the kitchen."

Mom led him down the hall.

KEY WORDS

- snap
- pull up (↔ pull down)
- sleepyhead
- fill with
- sunlight
- surprise
- lead (lead-led-led)

On the kitchen table were three presents.

They were a toy Troodon, a toy Triceratops, and a toy Spinosaurus.

Milton scooped them in his arms.

"Tory! Cera! Spiny!

Thank you, Mom and Dad!"

Dad chuckled.

"We decided you could have some dinosaurs.

Just not real dinosaurs."

"You look tired," Mom said to Milton.

"If I didn't know better, I would think you had been up all night playing."

Milton smiled.

He would never, ever, ever tell about Dinosaur Island.

Would you?

KEY WORDS

- present
- scoop
- chuckle
- decide

- tired
- better
- be up all night

A Put the sentences in order.

❶ Mom led Milton down the hall.

❷ Mom pulled up the window shade.

❸ "We have a surprise for you," Dad said.

❹ Mom said, "Wake up, sleepyhead!"

__________ → __________ → __________ → __________

B Choose the best answer to each question.

❶ Why did Troodon say he could NOT play jump rope at recess?

a) His claws were too long.

b) He did not like recess.

c) He did not know how to play jump rope.

d) He would scare the children.

❷ Why did Troodon tell Milton to keep Dinosaur Island a secret?

a) It would be too crowded if everyone came to the island.

b) People would trap the dinosaurs if they found the island.

c) Dinosaur Island is too dangerous for others.

d) Troodon did not tell him to keep a secret.

Solve the crossword puzzle.

Across

❸ Milton's parents gave him _________ presents.

❺ Milton asked Troodon to play jump _________.

Down

❶ Troodon said dinosaurs do not like to be _________ at school.

❷ Milton asked Troodon to be his _________.

❹ Milton crossed his _________ with his finger.

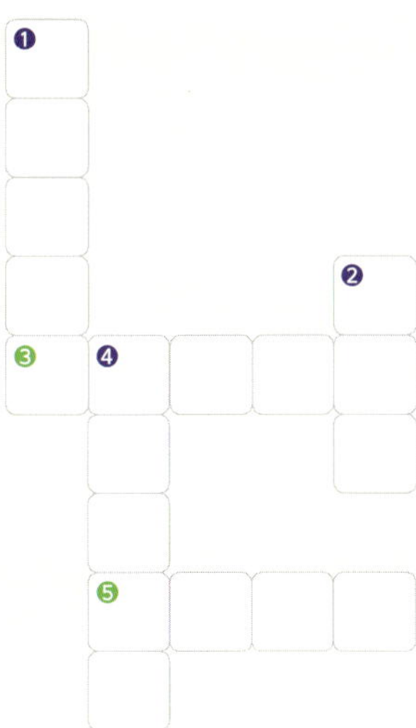

Fill in the blanks to review the story.

Title: The Night with the ______

Summary:

Milton wants a ______ for a pet. His parents say no. He reads a book about dinosaurs and goes to s______. A Troodon comes to Milton's bedroom w______. He takes Milton to Dinosaur ______. Milton meets many dinosaurs. Milton makes a promise to keep Dinosaur Island a ______. For his b______, his parents give him ______ dinosaurs.

Facts about Dinosaurs:

- **Troodon:** Its teeth were s______ and jagged.

  It had the biggest ______ for its size.
- **Spinosaurus:** Its back feet were w______.

  It ate ______.

  It had a big ______ on its back.
- **Parasaurolophus:** It had a ______ on its head.

  It used the ______ like a t______.
- **Triceratops:** It ate p______.

  It had a s______ on its head.
- **Pteranodon:** It was a flying r______.

Let's Think & Talk

Think about the following questions and answer them freely.

❶ Among the dinosaurs in the book, which one do you like the most? If you went to Dinosaur Island with the dinosaur, what would you want to do? Think about your favorite dinosaur's characteristics, the reason why you like the dinosaur, and the things that you want to do on the island. After organizing your ideas, tell us what you think.

❷ What will happen if people bring dinosaurs back to life using science like in the movies *Jurassic Park* and *Jurassic World*? Can dinosaurs be our friends or only a threat to us? After organizing your ideas, tell us what you think.

❸ There are many extinct animals like dinosaurs in our living world. Why did they become extinct? Search for extinct animals other than dinosaurs and the reason why they became extinct.

Let's Review the Story

Title: The Night with the **Dinosaurs**

Summary:

Milton wants a **dinosaur** for a pet. His parents say no. He reads a book about dinosaurs and goes to **sleep**. A Troodon comes to Milton's bedroom **window**. He takes Milton to Dinosaur **Island**. Milton meets many dinosaurs. Milton makes a promise to keep Dinosaur Island a **secret**. For his **birthday**, his parents give him **toy** dinosaurs.

Facts about Dinosaurs:

- **Troodon:** Its teeth were **sharp** and jagged.

  It had the biggest **brain** for its size.
- **Spinosaurus:** Its back feet were **webbed**.

  It ate **fish**.

  It had a big **sail** on its back.
- **Parasaurolophus:** It had a **crest** on its head.

  It used the **crest** like a **trumpet**.
- **Triceratops:** It ate **plants**.

  It had a **shield** on its head.
- **Pteranodon:** It was a flying **reptile**.

- **The Night with the Dinosaurs**
- **Level 2**
- **18 Questions**

  (Vocabulary 5 / Reading Comprehension 10 /

  Sentence Structure & Grammar 3)

1. Which pair has the wrong past tense form of the listed verb?

   ① throw – threw   ② keep – kept

   ③ spread – spread   ④ lead – lead

2. Which pair has the wrong comparative form of the listed adjective?

   ① long → longer   ② big → bigger

   ③ fun → funer   ④ smart → smarter

3. Each word is a specific example of the word listed on the right side. Which one is an incorrect example?

   ① hamster → pet   ② trumpet → reptile

   ③ island → place   ④ magnolia → plant

4. What does "extinct" mean in the following sentence?

   Dinosaurs are <u>extinct</u>.

   ① very big

   ② died a long time ago

   ③ like to be warm

   ④ sleepy

5. What are the proper words for the blanks?

   - I will take the best care _____________ my dinosaur.
   - Milton had to run to keep up _____________ him.

   ① up – of   ② to – on

   ③ of – with   ④ with – at

6. What is the reason Milton cannot have a dinosaur?

① They live in museums.

② They are extinct.

③ They are too big.

④ They are too loud.

7. What are two things mentioned as Proganochelys' characteristics?

① a crest on her head

② spikes on her neck

③ a sharp tail

④ long, sharp teeth

8. How do we know Troodon was the smartest dinosaur?

① It could talk.

② It could read.

③ No one knows for sure.

④ It had the biggest brain of all the dinosaurs for its size.

9. What things did Triceratops like to eat?

① other dinosaurs

② insects

③ plants

④ fish

10. How big was the pterosaur?

① as big as a jet airplane

② as big as a paper airplane

③ as big as Tyrannosaurus Rex

④ as big as Milton

11. Where was the pterosaur's nest?

① in a big palm tree

② on the ground

③ in a cave

④ under the water

12. What is NOT right about Pteranodon?

① It had leathery wings.

② It was two meters tall.

③ Its wingspan was ten meters wide.

④ It had five fingers.

13. How did Milton show he could keep a secret?

① He held up two fingers.

② He closed his eyes.

③ He shook hands with Tory.

④ He crossed his heart with his finger.

14. Where does Troodon think that adults will lock them up if adults find their island?

① in jail

② in a museum

③ in a zoo

④ in a circus

15. What did Milton get for his birthday?

① a toy Troodon, Triceratops, and Spinosaurus

② a toy Troodon, T-Rex, and Pteranodon

③ a toy Troodon, Tyrannosaurus Rex, and Spinosaurus

④ a toy Parasaurolophus, Spinosaurus, and Tyrannosaurus Rex

16.

It <u>is</u> <u>very</u> <u>bigger</u> <u>than</u> a shark's fin.
① ② ③ ④

17.

You wouldn't <u>be</u> able <u>to</u> <u>running</u> free <u>and</u> wild.
① ② ③ ④

18. What is the right sentence?

① He hear the trees move.
② He is hearing the trees to move.
③ He heard the trees move.
④ He was hearing the trees to move.

Memo

Memo

Memo 

Memo

Suzanne Pitner
Suzanne Pitner is a teacher and writer who has enjoyed visiting Alaska, exploring Rome, teaching in China, and is looking forward to more world travel. She has a Master's Degree in Education, and is a graduate of the Long Ridge Writer's Group. In addition to writing educational articles and books, she writes historical fiction and contemporary fiction for young adults using the pen name Suzanne Lilly.

The Night with the Dinosaurs

Written by Suzanne Pitner
Illustrated by Gyeongho Jeong

First Published in December 2015

Editorial Manager: Juyon Choi
Editors: Kyunghee Jang, Jiyeong Park
Designers: Eunhee Lee, Elim
Cover Designer: Eunhee Lee

Published and distributed by

Darakwon Bldg., 64-1 Jandari-ro, Mapo-gu, Seoul, Korea 04031
Tel: 82-2-736-2031(ext. 250)   Fax: 82-2-732-2037
Homepage: www.ihappyhouse.co.kr
Publisher: Kyudo Chung

ISBN: 978-89-6653-214-8 18740 / 978-89-6653-156-1 18740(set)

[Components]
• 1 Audio CD (Recording Studio: Aram)
• Answer Keys & Korean Translation: Free download at www.ihappyhouse.co.kr